Edelweiss

*Chronicle of a Del Mar Beach House
1885 to Now*

Juliana Maxey-Allison

Dayton Publishing LLC
P. O. Box 1521
Solana Beach, CA 92075
858-254-2959
publisher@daytonpublishing.com

ISBN-13: 978-0-9970032-0-8

To Edelweiss
and those who have lived there,
past and present

Acknowledgments

*First: my grateful appreciation to the Del Mar Historical Society
for generously sharing the wonderful vintage photographs reproduced here
under the guidance of Larry Brooks, who also helped keep the prose accurate;
to Abigail Maxey, whose lovely illustrations complete the picture;
and to Linnea Dayton who agreed to edit and publish this edition.*

*And: my sincere thank you to Barbara Allison, who helped get this started;
to my daughter Elizabeth Zusev, a photographer whose work appears here;
to my granddaughter Isabella, who drew the ice cream cone;
to David Maxey for agreeing to buy a shabby shack all those years ago;
and to my husband Brad, who keeps it all young.*

Contents

In this photo of Edelweiss, the east-side "greenhouse" can be seen on the left, and the front entrance on the north side, with stairs, is at the right. When I encountered the house in 1972, it didn't look fundamentally different. Just dilapidated and abandoned.

1
The Appeal

On a whim, I took a look at an "old Victorian beach cottage" on 10th Street one early Fall afternoon in 1972, when I was young and new to Del Mar. "Old Victorian beach cottage" was intriguing.

The key word, I soon saw, was "old." This cottage looked its age. Bright and new in 1885 at the start of Del Mar, it now sagged, it slouched, its white paint now patched and grayed, its right angles all askew. Actually, there weren't any right angles left.

A dreamy-looking glass greenhouse leaned in on the east side. High up on the outside of the west wall, large faded red capital letters spelled **EDELWEISS**.

In front, ancient shaggy jade plants, their tops frosted with flaked-off paint, stood guard like Asian palace dogs. The rest of the yard was an abandoned landscape of long-dead dusty tufts, squatting beneath two rusted cedar trees. Two Torrey pines were separated on lots to the west and east.

Dappled sunlight lit the house. It was charming and compelling. I took the next step, steps, up rickety stairs onto the enclosed front porch. Everything was off-kilter. Everything teetered and squeaked.

Inside, all was silent, sepia-toned, spooky, empty with a kind of hang-dog haunted look, dust flecks flickering on shafts of light. Not a Victorian fantasy. Any plush clutter, any original flourishes were long gone. No velvets. No fringe. No chandeliers, no stained glass windows. No frills. Nothing fussy. No carving or inlay. Only old wood.

And it might be for sale.

2
Psychology Today *in Del Mar*

I had just settled into a quite nice new white-walled condo sitting on the bluffs in Solana Beach, after looking at many, many houses with my husband David Maxey, and our two-year-old son, Brian. We were here from Manhattan, moved to the neighborhood because David was now the editor of the recently launched magazine *Psychology Today,* or *PT,* that Nicolas Charney had thought up as a graduate student in Psychology at the budding UCSD campus, opened in 1960. Charney, in his early 20s, first worked on *PT* while living in the guest house of Judy and Walter Munk, the distinguished professor at the Scripps Institution of Oceanography. Soon *PT* needed space and opened offices in Del Mar, a choice close to the expanding campus.

At this tail end of the pre-digital days, books, magazines and newspapers were still only printed on paper, and phones only existed with physically grounded land lines, as we and the country absorbed the new realities of the civil rights movement, the anti–Vietnam War protests, the rise of a feminist dialogue, hippie counterculture and fashion, relaxed sexual attitudes, experimental drugs, psychedelic art and music, running, surfing, biking and psychology. It all played out in Del Mar.

PT was an immediate hit. Readers responded. They subscribed to the magazine because of the interpretive articles that translated innovative research findings and developments in psychology from academic-speak into easily readable prose. The words were further clarified by bold graphic design. Psychology PhDs, some just graduated, were drawn by the gamble, the newness, the frenzied energy, the casual dress, the dune buggies, the ocean, and experienced editors and art directors. They squeezed into offices scattered all over Del Mar.

Building upon the dizzying success of *PT,* the startup company, CRM (for Communications, Research, Machines and for founders Charney, Reynolds and Marston), ambitiously added newsletters, books, games, even a movie division, renting more and more square footage to house the projects. More people squeezed in. If meetings got too crowded, the group moved on to a restaurant or the beach. The atmosphere was exhilarating and someone new was always arriving to experience this West Coast whirl.

Famous and adventurous people swept in and out to work and party, to be part of the mix of psychiatrists, psychologists, academics, business people, marketing people, support staff, all categories of consultants, and San Diego celebs of the day, including Theodore Geisel (Dr. Seuss), Jonas Salk with his institute designed by architect Louis Kahn in 1962, Françoise Gilot, Neil Morgan, Mary Walshok and Peter Drucker.

CRM became the city's biggest employer, ever.

The cover of Psychology Today, Vol. 1, No. 1 *(in 1967) made it clear this publication took a new and different approach to reporting developments in psychology research.* PT's *popularity with readers gave rise to a growth industry that greatly influenced the development of Del Mar.*

3
The Del Mar Way

el Mar, incorporated as an independent city in 1959, was still a spot on the way to somewhere else in the early '70s when I got there, a convenience stop, an upscale 7/11 sprawled along Old Highway 101 with its grocery store, drug store, book store, restaurants, auto shops, and a string of nine (9!) gas stations, with plenty of street parking. A few grand homes evoked the city's high-glam history, but most were modest, frilled-out with lush Southern California plantings.

As CRM divisions spread out into Del Mar, major transformations shaped the city's fringes. The Salk Institute and UCSD drew academic stars and students. Some settled in Del Mar or into the just developed Del Mar Heights homes. Carmel Valley, empty and wild, was on the brink of being built. The Golden State Freeway, Interstate 5, had opened to give drivers a fast-moving alternative to Highway 101.

In the 1970s the street scene on Del Mar's Highway 101, or Camino Del Mar, reflected the prosperity and laid-back lifestyle of the town.

4
Decision: The Broken House

Inside the old Victorian beach cottage not much had changed in recent years. The house's original 12-foot-tall tongue-in-groove boards of rough-sawn redwood still stood in the mode of the single-wall construction of 1885. I could see the ocean through the slots where some of the planks had separated, as easily as I could see out of the windows. The milled ceiling and window details, more formal than the walls themselves, were solid. The floor was not. It was rough, barnlike.

Four doors opened directly to the outside. Within, door after door led to odd small spaces. Some were closet-size, some actual rooms. They were bare.

So was the kitchen. No appliances, no shelves, just bits of plumbing parts dangling like broken jewelry where some sort of sink had sat. That floor was worse, worn to splinters.

Farther on, in a tiny tacked-on shack, a bleak broken toilet, angled into a corner, shared space with a cracked sink. Happily, it didn't smell funny.

That glass greenhouse-like attraction on the east side of the house was, up close, a randomly rigged jumble of reclaimed windows that overran the property line.

Young Brian, summing up, pronounced the whole the "broken house." Indeed. Hard to figure how people in the past, and the very recent past, had managed living in Edelweiss.

But it was just a jaunt to the *PT* offices on Camino Del Mar in one direction and to a great beach in the other. Who could resist?

Busy with his new job at *PT*, David eyed Edelweiss, antique, unique, admittedly more ready for a wrecking crew than a restoration.

After a bit of persuading, he drew in a deep breath and agreed to the project, as long as he wasn't involved. At all.

We bought Edelweiss, which wasn't quite on the market yet, in December, 1972, for $30,000. David went off to his office. I headed to 10th Street.

The perfect beach was five blocks away. And Camino Del Mar, the town's main street, was just up 10th Street.

David, Julie and Brian Maxey. We were young and energetic, and at least one of us was enthusiastic about restoring Edelweiss.

5
Del Mar's Backstory

In the early 1880s Jacob Shell Taylor grasped the potential impact the burgeoning technology of locomotion could have on the town of Weed — the area that would later become Del Mar. By that time the state of California already had quite a history.

Spain had claimed the native American Indian land in the 1500s, and in the 1700s had busily constructed a series of mission settlements some 30 miles apart, a day's walk for the padres, on El Camino Real. The route that connected the missions started in San Diego and headed north for 650 miles up to Sonoma, curving inland in some places, skipping the coastal mix of mesas and marshes. This route, first traveled by foot, horseback, mule and stagecoach, is still well used, as are many of the missions.

In a series of quick changes, Mexico took the territory for a time after the 1821 War of Independence with Spain, but lost it to the young United States of America in the 1848 Mexican-American War. That war brought Americans west to the area to fight. The resulting Treaty of Guadalupe Hidalgo annexed California and other western territories to the United States. Though this sizable chunk of land was a long and rugged struggle from the established eastern states, it lured adventuring pioneers. To explore and homestead the vast open spaces, they journeyed west along the Oregon Trail, some surviving, some not.

The 1849 discovery of gold at Sutter's Mill in Coloma, up north, catapulted California onto the national map. Fortune seekers, the '49ers, fueled by high hopes of easy nuggets, crossed the big country any way they could — by mule, on horseback, by horse and wagon.

The discovery of gold in California sped up the migration of Americans to the West Coast.

Some sailed all the way around Cape Horn, taking four months or more, to stake their claims at the mines.

Gold-rich California was quickly granted statehood, anchoring the West Coast to the United States. California was admitted as a non-slave state as part of the Congressional Compromise of 1850, which attempted to calm a raging national debate that centered on the status of slaves, and which may have stalled the Civil War for a few years. When the fighting finally flared in the 1860s, the Union's efforts were financed in part by funds from gold in San Francisco banks.

The Civil War spurred Congress' passage of the Pacific Railway Act of 1862 as a military necessity. As a result, trains opened the way westward. After years of haggling, route rights were resolved, and by the 1870s tracks had been laid for steam engines to cross the country from the East to Sacramento and San Francisco. This involved an army of engineers to negotiate gravity, trails, mountains, canyons, streets and streams, as well as the steel gangs, section men, bridge builders, carpenters, tie makers and other workers who put it all in place.

Travelers, weary of and worn from the rigors of rough trails and high seas, traded up to relatively rapid transit and the romance of the rails. A cross-country trip took only a week.

However, the California that was now connected to the East was up north. Without the glitter of gold, Southern California stayed isolated, island-like, surrounded by the formidable geography of massive mountains, vast deserts, primitive roads and the Pacific Ocean.

It was the 1880s before trains carried passengers over prairie lands, between blasted-out mountain gaps, through expanses of unwatered wilderness by the side of the Pacific Ocean, to the area called Weed in honor of William Weed, who owned most of it.

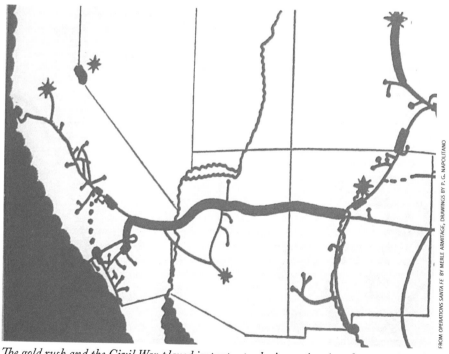

The gold rush and the Civil War played important roles in motivating the extension of railroad lines to California. The train tracks went first to San Francisco and Sacramento in the north, later to Los Angeles, and then to Del Mar and San Diego.

9

6

Taylor's Gamble: Weed to Del Mar

Jacob Shell Taylor, who had first landed in Julian, watched his friend Theodore Loop of Los Peñasquitos broker a deal to potentially bring a train depot into the town of Weed on the Pacific Ocean. A 6-foot-tall, 200+-pound Texan, Taylor had allegedly roamed around the West as an Indian scout for Buffalo Bill Cody.

Jacob Taylor was Del Mar's first developer.

In Weed, Taylor sized up the scrappy site and gambled that trains would soon bring people to the coast. In two separate transactions, he bought a total of 338 acres for $1000 in gold. (Manhattan Island was cheaper, but that was earlier.)

Taylor dreamed up an extravagant tourist destination and turned the raw territory into one, which he called Del Mar, the name Ella Loop, wife of Theodore, had given the area. Taylor cleared critters, brush and cacti, plotted out his city on a grid with wide roadways, built it and awaited new arrivals. Del Mar's grand attraction was Taylor's prize project, the Casa Del Mar, on 10th Street off Railroad Avenue just steps from the 9th Street train depot, choice for tourists.

Taylor marketed his luxurious resort as the "Newport of Southern California," referencing the majestic waterfront mansions, or "summer cottages," for the really quite rich in Newport, Rhode Island. Taylor built 14 more modest Mission-style houses for new residents, each with four rooms and eight-foot-high ceilings. His lots were $100, a lot with a house $600, and he probably rented some to staff for the hotel.

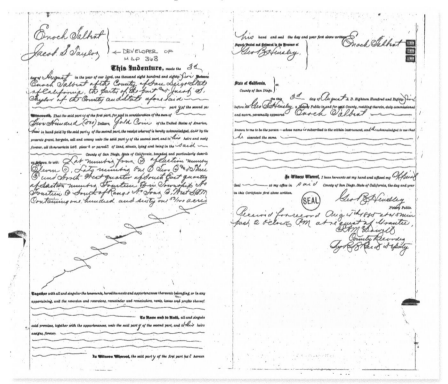

The deed for one half of Taylor's purchase of the land he would develop into Del Mar

11

People did train to Del Mar to see new sights, to have a good time or to take in the therapeutic air believed to ease upper respiratory troubles. Some came to find work, some to reinvent their lives — for as many reasons as there were arrivals. The railroad made this city a reality, as well as many another town along the California coast. Tourists, adventurers, ranchers, farmers, preachers, business people, hucksters,

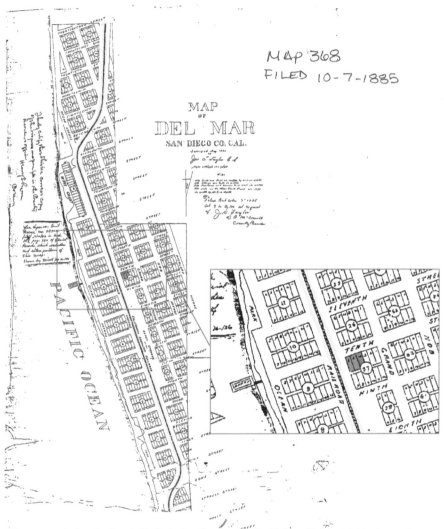

The original plan for Jacob Taylor's development of Del Mar, filed in 1885, shows the importance of the railroad line. The general location where the Edelweiss house was built is shown in green in the inset. A few years later the train tracks would be moved to the west, and the 100-foot-wide Railroad Avenue would be narrowed to become Stratford Court.

real estate developers, contractors, professional women and sheriffs arrived along with the Chinese train workers.

Del Mar grew. Taylor gave the town wooden sidewalks and street-lights as people moved in, bought lots and built houses. Tenth Street starred as the center of Del Mar when it came alive as a fantastic resort town in 1885, when the State of California was just 35 years old.

The Casa Del Mar hotel (top), shown here just before it opened in 1886, was convenient to the train station, seen here in a photo taken c. 1890.

Practical Taylor planted crops for the resort's dining room. He landscaped his city with white Castilian rose bushes and groves of eucalyptus, and he set cypress trees among the existing cedars and rare Torrey pines that clung to sandstone ridges, thriving on foggy mists.

Just a year after the town of Del Mar was begun, many of Jacob Taylor's lots were sold and filled with houses. Trees and sidewalks were not far behind. This photo shows the view looking west down 10th Street from a position a little west of what later came to be called Edelweiss house.

The Torrey Pine

Torrey pines are quite rare and site-specific, growing only in the Del Mar area and on Santa Rosa Island, southwest of Santa Barbara. In 1850 surgeon and botanist Dr. Charles Christopher Parry studied the scruffy pine, an Ice Age relict. Local people had known the tree many years before that, and 16th-century Spanish mariners had marked the area as a navigational aid, calling it Punta de Los Arboles, or "point of trees." But no one had formally classified the pine until Parry, who honored his mentor John Torrey by naming it *Pinus torreyana*, Torrey pine.

The Torrey Pines State Reserve was established in 1959 to protect the long-recognized "point of trees." When we moved in, Edelweiss house stood between two Torrey pines.

7

The Short, Sweet Life of the Casa Del Mar

Jacob Taylor's list of "Things To Do" in Del Mar and at his Casa Del Mar advertised walking, fishing, hunting, dancing, listening to musical recitals, playing cards, watching horse races on the beach and swimming. A stairway across the cliffs at 10th Street led down to a 350-by-40-foot natatorium built right out into the ocean to screen off bathers from rip currents and sting rays. Fun! The rates at this glamorous and popular resort were $2 per day, $9–$10 per week.

According to the *San Diego Union* newspaper, September 6, 1885:

> The town as laid out is situated on the line of the railroad, on the top of a cliff about 75 feet above the sea, and extends along the cliff two miles and back on the mesa half a mile, and is laid out in blocks 300 feet square with 20-foot alleys running through the blocks. The lots are 50 feet front by 140 feet deep. The streets are 100 feet wide and the cottages which have been built are 25 feet back from the street which makes 150 feet space, and when the trees have been planted and more houses put up, the town will be beautiful indeed.

It was, it glowed, but briefly.

Everything was coming up Castilian roses. Tourists trained in. The population ballooned. Investors and speculators triggered the region's first real estate boom.

Then, devastation.

DEL ☆ MAR

BY ☆ THE ☆ SEA.

BATHING POOL AT DEL MAR, CAL.

THE NEWPORT OF SOUTHERN CALIFORNIA!
THE MOST BEAUTIFUL MESA ON THE COAST.

Every Square a Pleasure Ground. A Semi-Tropical Picture from the Heights to the Beach.

The "Casa Del Mar"

COMBINES THE COMFORTS OF A HOME,
THE ELEGANCE OF A PALACE,
THE ROMANCE OF A SWISS COTTAGE,
THE AMUSEMENTS OF A BRILLIANT PLEASURE RESORT.

A Poem!   **A PANORAMA!**   A Realistic Picture
A Comedy!   in a Dream!

The only **Bathing Pool** directly in the Surf of the Pacific.

ARTISTIC COTTAGES FOR RENT.

☞THE TOURISTS' HEADQUARTERS.☜

Game Plentiful.   A Hunting Range in the Back Country.   Delightful Drives.

J. S. TAYLOR, PROPRIETOR,
Del Mar, California.

Taylor's description of the pleasures that awaited at Casa Del Mar

8

Boom to Bust

Maverick rains drenched Del Mar in February, 1884, then struck again, stronger, in 1888 when fierce storm waters ripped out railroad tracks, trees and crops, drowned livestock and smothered the wooden sidewalks with mud. Tourists vanished. Businesses shut. Residents digging out of the gummy mess faced dreary days dragged down by a weak economy. Some moved on, dismantled their houses and took the wood with them. Worse, a fire burned the Casa Del Mar and Taylor's dreams to ash in January, 1890, though a shift in the winds saved the rest of the town.

Grim, but it was part of a pattern of romance colliding with reality that underlies the boom and bust cycle threading through California's history. Taylor collected the insurance money, moved on to Texas and started anew, successfully.

Times stayed tough in Del Mar as the 1800s turned into the 1900s. Elsewhere Geronimo's surrender ended the last big war between the United States and native Americans, the Statue of Liberty was dedicated, the American Federation of Labor formed and Coca Cola was bottled, sporting real cocaine in its secret recipe. Mr. Ford was at work on his automobiles, Mr. Benz got a patent on the first gas-driven car, the Wright brothers imagined and designed flying machines, Sigmund Freud opened his practice and Mark Twain wrote. The Hotel Del Coronado was completed, as were several Southern California beach developments paralleling the coastal train routes.

After two years of flooding and a fire that destroyed the town's centerpiece resort hotel, some residents of Del Mar gave up and moved on, and times were hard for many of those who remained.

9

Fast Forward

All the years later, when we bought the house late in 1972, Edelweiss was rooted on the middle lot of its original three. The west lot had been sold off and was home to two residential condominiums. The east lot was vacant.

Although the house had been built on Taylor's north-south grid, the architecture, footprint and ceiling height differed from his favored Mission style. It was more East Coast than West, even early West Coast, maybe because the first owner, Franklin West, was from Nova Scotia.

Some of the floor, support wood and trim — oak and Douglas fir — had been milled. The 12-foot-tall rough-sawn redwood walls had come from Northern California's old-growth trees (2000! years old).

The front room expanded to side rooms, east and west. No hallways. All the inside doors opened directly to rooms and strange tight spaces. No plaster, but patterned papers had been pasted to some of the walls.

There was a single small bathroom, obviously built long ago, probably to replace the outhouse, which was of course long gone.

We wouldn't learn about the separate origin of the porch, the "greenhouse," the gingerbread trim or the Edelweiss name until I researched the history of the house later on. Or that there had once been a stable and an alley dump. At this point in 1972, all we knew was that it was going to take major rebuilding to make this spot our home.

I couldn't wait to get started.

Originally centered on three of Taylor's lots, in 1972 Edelweiss house occupied only the lot in the middle. And two lots had been added to the west of that block of 10th Street after Railroad Avenue was narrowed to become Stratford Court.

10
Reboot

F irst, I interviewed architects. One wanted to lower the ceiling and
cover the walls with sheet rock. One wanted to tear the house
down and put two houses on the R-2–zoned lot that would allow
two dwellings. Practical ideas. I, young, with less than zero experience, wanted old Edelweiss original, but with modern touches such as
electricity, plumbing, heat, a kitchen and bathrooms, and solid outside
walls. I wanted the backyard, not another neighbor. The architect we
chose, George Margine of La Jolla, got it. For the permit application
he produced elegant plans with precise instructions down to the nail
sizes.

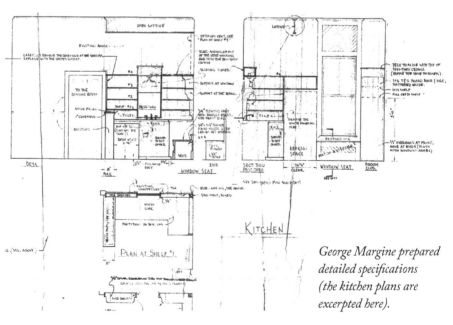

*George Margine prepared
detailed specifications
(the kitchen plans are
excerpted here).*

I got approval from San Diego County to rebuild it. I never even thought to apply to the city of Del Mar. I never knew that I should. No one from the city said a word to us, though our efforts were in plain sight as we jacked up Edelweiss, straightened it out and totally rebuilt it.

Probably people expected it to be torn down and replaced with a couple of condos. In time it may be, as is happening with many Del Mar properties.

We were an eclectic lot: a lead carpenter, key skilled workers, a roundup of scraggly UCSD PhD candidates in Philosophy, brother Jack Guenther plus his ready rugby-player buddies, and anyone else who would work, along with a cat that came with the house and that we called Mamoo.

We propped the house up and went to work on it. Here carpenter Ken Hellingson studies the plans. Mamoo the cat supervised.

23

The men favored working on the west side for the view. The ocean, sure, but the bigger draw was our long-legged bikini-clad neighbor, who sunned herself daily. During all this work we dug up lots of bones. I don't think any were human.

We worked within the 1885 shell and the 1905 porch. We kept the Douglas fir framing, the 12-foot-tall redwood walls and the window placements.

I found a lumberyard in San Diego able to match the mill work where we needed it. We left an obscure trace of antique wallpaper lingering in a slot in the middle room. The floor restorer who said he could do magic did. We outfitted two closet-sized spaces as bathrooms and reconstructed the one in the back. We fitted out a kitchen and put tile down to replace the savaged floor. We wrapped the newly plumbed and electrified house with insulation then wrapped the insulation in an outer layer of wood. Then we roofed it and added central heat.

Plans, lumber, and floor restoration

24

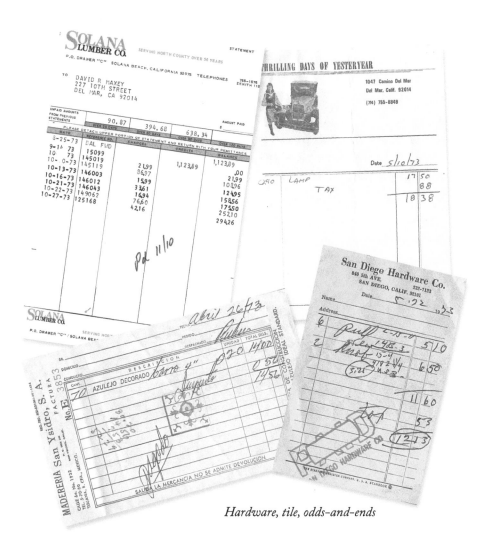

Hardware, tile, odds-and-ends

We reproduced the curly trim and diamond-shaped cutouts on the porch that had been added in 1905. We painted the house a clean white and commissioned an artist to originate an Edelweiss sign, this time in blue.

KRISTINA KREFTING

Things got done. Dumb luck, naive optimism and a willing architect, no practical knowledge or experience on my part, moved us along. The small reversals got resolved, except once: When returning to the house, I heard an odd, eerie wind whistle whose origin I never discovered, detached, like a signal, a warning. It was. Two lovely old moon-shaped beveled glass windows from the pile that was the greenhouse were gone, and so was the wrought iron front gate.

As an afterthought we fitted out "the mansion," a small on-site outbuilding, to be our tiny guest room with bathroom.

We set up a sandbox for Brian in the big backyard along with the old California pepper trees, new grass and a little lemon tree. We planted African daisies in the front yard under the two grayed cedars. The Torrey pine trees that had been planted years before on either side of the house now grew on separate lots.

"The mansion" before renovation (top left) and as it appears today (bottom right). Guests of Barbra Dillenger who visited in intervening years made paintings of this little building.

11
Living in Edelweiss

W e moved in. We had good times at the beach, fishing, getting to know people and entertaining and partying with the various characters and psychiatrist celebrities associated with *Psychology Today* and our family.

In the early 1970s we enjoyed Edelweiss with visiting friends and family.

We were too busy or too noisy to wonder about any past people, ghosts or spirits of former inhabitants that might be lurking, though we sometimes heard odd sounds at night, and pictures did fall off the wall. We heard juicy rumors that the famous movie stars Mary Pickford and Douglas Fairbanks stayed in the house in the 1920s and still visited. I wondered what they did and where.

12
While We Were Away

Psychology Today, too fresh and successful not to get noticed, was bought by New York publisher Ziff Davis, who packed up the magazine and anyone who wanted to go off to Manhattan in 1975. Boomeranging back to friends we had left to move west, we lived in New York City, where our daughter Elizabeth was born.

When David Maxey died in 1984, our home was in New York, settled in our big, bright Upper West Side apartment, the Belnord, 1908. With Brian in school and Elizabeth in preschool, and with plenty of disruption in our lives already, we stayed for stability.

The Belnord today looks much as it did when we lived there.

PUCCI MCGILL

When we had left Del Mar, I had rented Edelweiss first to best forgotten tenants whose off-culture antics I don't want to retell, and then to my brother, who knew the house so well. Brian and Elizabeth would stop in to see Uncle Jack at Edelweiss on summer trips to visit their Grandmother Elba.

A ride in a New York taxi was the first step as Brian and Elizabeth began one of their visits to Grandmother Elba in her waterfront condo in Oceanside and to Uncle Jack at Edelweiss.

When Jack moved on, Barbra Dillenger and Michael Makay took tender care of Edelweiss. The transpersonal counselors ran their business and held many meetings and conferences in the house. Barbra often sensed the presence of people from past years, including Mary Pickford and Douglas Fairbanks, and occasionally smelled a scent from a perfume or powder from earlier times.

They also recalled passersby who stopped, even wandered in, to ask if the house was a bed and breakfast or a store. One even asked the price of their furniture.

At Edelweiss Barbra Dillenger and Michael Makay felt the presence of life in bygone days.

13
Circling Back

M y husband Bradford Allison and I moved to 10th Street in
2004. A few houses on the street date from Del Mar's early
history, when it was the most important street at the very center of
the resort town. Two residential condominiums now cover what was
the east lot of the Edelweiss property. Almost endless housing and
shopping developments have paved over and tamed the wild lands.
UCSD, its Scripps Institution of Oceanography and the Salk Institute
almost constitute townships on their own. The disappearing cliffs are
ever more fragile, the ocean waters are rising and we as residents can
expect less fresh water. Yet I found Del Mar true to its roots: a beauti-
ful place on the planet. The beach town had returned to Taylor's early
vision of Del Mar as a destination on the ocean with a luxurious resort
attractive to visitors, celebrities and residents.

*Seawater on the west and
freshwater runoff from the
land continually reshape
Del Mar's picturesque
sandstone bluffs.*

14
Tracking Down History

Back at Edelweiss, I pieced together a patchwork collection of facts about the house's history from books, articles and local lore, but it wasn't such solid information. To track exactly who had owned and lived in Edelweiss and what their lives might have been like, I reviewed some records from San Diego County. This interesting exercise started well, but as they go back in time, the written records are not in any easily found sequence or even alphabetized, although the handwriting is artfully eloquent.

I wanted a real ghost from years past willing to pinpoint who had owned the house, tell all the secret tales and sort out the rumors

It would have been helpful to have a long-time resident spirit to fill me in on the inhabitants of Edelweiss over the years.

about celebrities who might have lived there. But it is hard to harness a phantom. Without that charmed insight, without in most cases descriptions of what these people might have looked like or what a person's private wishes, impulses and habits might have been, I had to resort to a title search for at least a trail of ordinary facts.

In 2009 I was lucky to learn more from two former neighbors who had grown up on 10th Street in the 1920s and had talked to others whose history is here. Largely from them, and from searches I was able to start because of what they were able to tell me, I put together the history of Edelweiss from 1885 to when I found it in 1972. Although it would have seemed unlikely to me at the outset of my search, most — from the second owner to the next-to-last — have been women. This pattern of ownership is probably a reflection of an interesting chapter in the history of California property law.

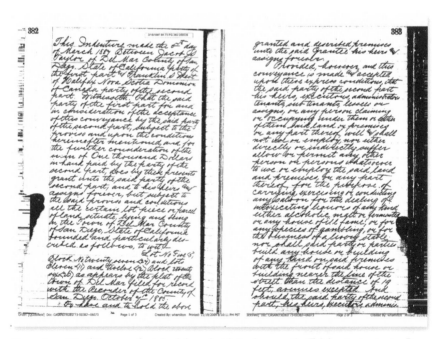

Pages 1 and 2 of the very first deed for what later became the Edelweiss property. It transferred three lots at the corner of 10th Street and Railroad Avenue from Jacob Taylor, the original developer, to Franklin West in 1887.

15
Owner #1: Franklin L. West
1887–1904

First, Franklin L. West of Nova Scotia gambled on Del Mar. How he learned about the new development is lost to time but a testament to Taylor's talent as a serious developer/promoter. Investor West bought three lots that formed the southeast corner of 10th Street and Railroad Avenue, now Stratford Court.

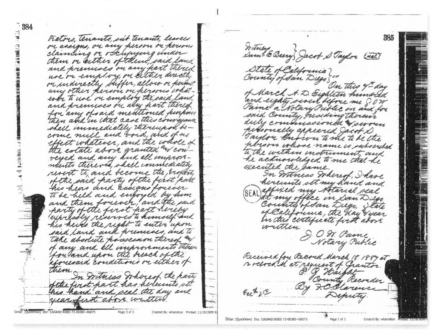

Pages 3 and 4 of the deed transferring three lots at the corner of 10th Street and Railroad Avenue from Jacob Taylor to Franklin West in 1887. Pages 1 and 2 are shown opposite, on page 32.

By 1887, maybe earlier, West had the house on the middle lot. It looked almost the same as it does now with its East Coast tone, except for the front porch and curly woodwork, which were added later. I couldn't locate a record of who actually built the house, or if Mr. West himself ever lived in it. He may have invested long-distance and had it built to his specs. He did rent it out. Maybe as a boarding house to men who worked for the railroad or helped build the town, or, maybe to women who ran their own business. The West was still on the wild side, and with all those working men there must have been a brothel somewhere.

The house on 10th Street would have been perfect. Lots of outside entrance doors, lots of inside doors to small spaces, plus a clearly convenient location. Just a thought.

Pure speculation: Artist's rendition of an early occupant of the house at 10th Street and Railroad Avenue

16
Del Mar's General Store

Whatever its earliest beginnings, historical records confirm that by the late 1880s the house was the town's General Merchandise Store, most likely a live/work setup with the managers on site. There was a back alley for deliveries, a dump, an outhouse, plus plenty of land on the side lots to stable horses and grow crops. Maybe the two Torrey pines on either side of the house got their start then.

By 1898 the Stelzner family was renting the house, both to live in and to operate as the General Store. Their small business on 10th Street blossomed as the city rose from the sad ashes of the Casa Del Mar. Business brightened again. By 1900 San Diego County's population had begun a steady rise that would continue into the following decades. People came from other parts of California. They came from the East and the Midwest. Europe had sagged under a severe economic depression in 1882, and many people, more than 250,000 of them, packed up to try their luck in the United States, mostly settling in the Midwest. People came to Del Mar from Iowa, Kansas, Nebraska, West Virginia, Texas, Pennsylvania, New Jersey, New York, France and Germany. Oscar Stelzner himself, 45, who listed his profession as "General Merchant," was from Germany; his wife, Elizabeth (Lizzie), also 45, was from New York, and her daughter, (his stepdaughter) Effie, 14, had been born in Illinois.

The Stelzners worked hard. They had little electricity, no helpful appliances, sketchy communications systems and difficult delivery routes. But a shopper's alternative was a trek to San Diego by rail, bicycle or eventually early auto over rutted dirt roads. The Stelzners did well.

17
Owner #2: Lizzie Stelzner
1904–1929

Entrepreneurial Lizzie Stelzner juggled being wife to Oscar and mother to her daughter, keeping the house in order, and managing the laundry of long dresses, many layers. The Stelzners probably had a garden to grow their edibles as well as ordering, organizing and selling staples and goods at the store.

Lizzie also got the designation of Del Mar Post Office for the place, with herself as postmistress. The 10th Street store was where

Our only early photo of Edelweiss is on a distressed 1907 postcard picturing local land-marks. In the center of these grouped pictures is Edelweiss.

one shopped, picked up mail and greeted neighbors. Busy Lizzie and Oscar must have known everybody's business.

In 1904 Lizzie bought the house on three lots from Franklin West for $350, taking title in her name only. That was when 10th Street was still the town's commercial center. She owned it until 1929, long after the center of Del Mar had shifted to 15th Street.

Lizzie was the first of a series of women owners of Edelweiss. Curious about why so many of the owners were women, I consulted a librarian at the San Diego History Center. I learned that in the early days of San Diego County it was not unusual for married couples to put the house title in the wife's name. In those days, women did not share the same property rights as men. If the house was in the wife's name and the husband died, she would not have to prove ownership in order to take possession, because the house already belonged to her. Whereas if she died, her husband could just claim his dead wife's property without obstacle.

A blowup of the central photo on the postcard opposite gives us a blurred and shadowy glimpse of Lizzie or Effie, or perhaps both.

18
Ice Cream & Swiss Styling

In 1905 Lizzie's daughter Effie married Horace Stolzy. He moved in. Lizzie and Oscar moved the General Store to 9th Street and moved their household into the Casa Alvarado at 144 10th Street (still standing today, albeit off-site, overseen by the Del Mar Historical Society).

Effie and Horace kept the original house commercial. They opened an ice cream parlor complete with a soda fountain and sold penny candies in the front room.

Gottesburen's General Store on 9th Street preceded the Stelzners' store on 10th Street. Later Oscar and Lizzie moved their store out of Edelweiss to a 9th Street location.

Sometime before 1907 they remodeled the outside of the house. They added the front porch with the distinguished diamond-shaped cutouts that wrapped all the way around the north and west sides. They put up the curly woodwork that rides up the edges of the steep roof lines. They painted "**EDELWEISS**" in big dark-red letters high up on the west side of the white house. The red and white colors were drawn from the Swiss flag in honor of Horace's native Switzerland.

Artist's rendition of the Edelweiss house, drawn from the distressed photo on the 1907 postcard of "Views of Del Mar," shown on page 36.

The Edelweiss Flower

Composers Richard Rodgers and Oscar Hammerstein, who weren't Swiss, wrote the song "Edelweiss" that celebrates the flower for their 1957 musical *The Sound of Music.* Edelweiss, "noble and white" *Leontopodium alpinum,* or Lion's foot, thrives upon the rocky crags and ledges of the European Alps. Romantic legends claim the bloom to be a "Love Charm of the Mountains," a talisman to ward off evil or a medical remedy. It is nice to think so, and Edelweiss is officially protected by the agreement of the International Conference of Alpine Clubs signed by Switzerland, Austria, Germany and Italy in 1878. Sadly, the flower doesn't do well in Del Mar, though maybe the name itself retains some of the magic.

Edelweiss in bloom

19
The Rise of 15th Street

As Edelweiss got its new look at the beginning of the 1900s, so did Del Mar. The South Coast Land Company, a syndicate from Los Angeles, came to town in 1905 and bought up a lot of it. Lizzie reckoned the company's arrival would be an opportunity to boost business at the 9th Street store.

That didn't happen. Instead the developers, who adopted Taylor's concept of Del Mar as a resort town, reset the city center from 10th to 15th Street. They built their luxurious hotel there — the Stratford Inn, a Tudor-style homage to the Stratford-on-Avon of Shakespeare's time, landscaped by the well-known horticulturist and landscape artist Kate Sessions — and created a commercial area in the new town center with their own General Store.

The South Coast Land Company built the popular Stratford Inn. Kate Sessions (shown here) did the landscape design.

They transplanted the train station from 9th to 17th Street, convenient to their hotel, and wiped out any remaining traces of Taylor's early Del Mar. Lizzie was out of business.

New residents bought the company's lots on streets winding up the hills to Crest Road, following early animal paths, and built fancy houses. Del Mar flourished.

The "Del Mar Castle" was designed by renowned San Diego architect Richard Requa and built in 1926 for the Marston family. This photo of the house on Avenida Primavera, one of the winding streets on the hill east of Camino Del Mar and north of 15th Street, was probably taken from an airplane in the late 1940s.

20
Star-Studded Del Mar

A s the Hollywood film industry came into focus about 1910, bringing entertainment from stage to screen, celebrities sprinkled Del Mar, and maybe even Edelweiss, with stardust. Early actors — including the still famous names Rudolph Valentino, Charlie Chaplin, Marion Davies and Pola Negri — and also Jack Dempsey stayed at the Stratford Inn, often traveling on to Tijuana, then a destination hot spot.

Douglas Fairbanks and Mary Pickford, actors and co-founders of United Artists Studios, filmed some movies locally in Balboa Park,

Douglas Fairbanks and Mary Pickford sometime between 1915 and 1923

PRINTS AND PHOTOGRAPHS DIVISION, U. S. LIBRARY OF CONGRESS, HARRIS & EWING PHOTOGRAPHERS

Del Mar and La Jolla. Rumor has it that Fairbanks, the dashing, hand-some, athletic leading man, and the sweet Mary Pickford, pretty and coy, called "the most popular girl in the world," often stayed at Edel-weiss.

Business slowed at the Edelweiss Ice Cream Parlor on 10th Street, no longer the city's main street, but at its edge. Effie and Horace, now parents of Anna Elizabeth and Charles, needed money. It could be the famous stars Fairbanks and Pickford rented the house as a hideaway early in their affair while they were married to other people. Or maybe they used Edelweiss as a beach house after they married in 1920. They could have driven in from their 800-acre Rancho Santa Fe home they hoped to but did not develop into "Rancho Zorro." It is now Fairbanks Ranch.

Pure fantasy: A "faked" photo, an imagining of what might have been, on a spoof of the front page of the November 20, 1924 San Diego Union. As the ersatz caption tells us, shown left to right are Douglas Fairbanks, Charlotte Smith, Mary Pickford and Charlie Chaplin at Edelweiss.

21
Owners #3: Effie Stolzy & Children
1929–1934

In 1929 the stock market crashed, the Great Depression spread and Lizzie died. She willed Effie two-thirds of the ownership of Edelweiss, and gave the other one-third to her grandchildren. The property had gained some land across its southern boundary when the alley for that block was closed by San Diego County in 1929. But Effie and Horace faced drooping finances, an aging Edelweiss and their own private demons.

EXHIBIT "A"

Lot 5 in Block 27 of Del Mar, in the County of San Diego, State of California, according to the Map thereof No. 368, filed in the Office of the Recorder of said San Diego County October 7, 1885.

Also that portion of the Southerly 20.00 feet to Tenth Street, lying Northerly of and adjoining said Lot 5 as vacated and closed to public use by an Order of the Board of Supervisors of said San Diego County, April 12, 1926, a certified copy of said vacation having been recorded on April 16, 1926 in Book 1209, page 125 of Deeds, records of said San Diego County.

Also all that portion of the Northerly half of the alley in said Block 27, lying Southerly of and adjoining said Lot 5, as vacated and closed to public use on May 13, 1929 by an Order of the Board of Supervisors of said San Diego County and filed for record in Book 59, page 383 of Supervisors' records, a certified copy of said vacation having been filed for record on May 17, 1929 in Book 1613, page 470 of Deeds, records of said San Diego County.

The Edelweiss property grew when the back alley was closed.

45

22
Neighbors' Memories

Two of the Stolzys' neighbors who grew up on 10th Street remembered the Stolzy family and the Depression-era Edelweiss. Ernie Bertoncini lived across the street and played games and trains at Edelweiss with Effie's children, Anna and Charlie. He bought his penny candy from the store in the front room.

His sister Esther, five years old at the time, was chosen for a bit part in the 1914 movie *Hearts Adrift* that was shot in La Jolla and starred Mary Pickford, adding fat to the rumor that Mary and Doug stayed at Edelweiss.

"I was in the movie with Mary Pickford when I was a little girl," Esther said in a 1970s interview I found in the Del Mar library. "It was taken in La Jolla: *Hearts Adrift*. She stayed at the hotel [Stratford Inn]. Mary Pickford was so lovely and said she'd been in the movies since she was five years old."

Hearts Adrift was a silent short romance released in 1914 starring Mary Pickford. The film is no longer known to exist in studio or public archives or in private collections.

46

When I interviewed Ernie at Edelweiss in 2009, he pointed to the spot in the front room where Horace sat in his rocking chair reading racing forms, getting set to bet via courier on the horses running at Tijuana's Agua Caliente, the racetrack of the era. Horace's bets turned bad. According to Ernie, "Horace lost the house in a gambling debt. Effie went crazy."

Bill Arballo, the well-known journalist and a former mayor of Del Mar, recalled with horror his visit to look at Edelweiss by his parents' side in 1933. Corroborating Ernie's report, he said, "The house was in total disrepair. The porch was dank with sea grass growing over it."

No sale. The Arballos settled instead on a house down the street known as Casa Alvarado, or the Alvarado House — the house where Lizzie and Oscar Stelzner moved when their daughter and her husband moved into Edelweiss. The Alvarado House is now under the care of the Del Mar Historical Society. The Arballos grew watermelons and pomegranates. Bill played baseball with friends on the diamond on 9th Street.

The Arballo family turned down the opportunity to buy the distressed Edelweiss, instead settling in the Alvarado House at 144 10th Street. One of the original 1885 houses in Jacob Taylor's Del Mar, the building was later moved to the city hall parking lot and then to the Del Mar Fairgrounds to preserve it. As the new civic center is built, the Del Mar Historical Society hopes to settle the house there, near its original site.

23
Owner #4: Lida Scripps
1934–1944

During this dark time for the Stolzy family, a Ms. Lida Scripps took title. Lida Scripps was 78 years old when she bought Edelweiss and its rotting porch with sodden sea grass growing into it, for $1. I wonder how and why. Did she actually win it gambling? Did she simply agree to take it over? Whatever the impetus, Effie first paid her children $10 for their one-third ownership, and then Lida paid Effie $1 for the house. Odd.

Lida, a member of the elite La Jolla Beach & Tennis Club, owned other property in California and the Midwest but was short on cash. At one point, when she was hospitalized after an automobile accident, a friend appealed on her behalf to the Ellen Browning Scripps relief trust fund. Though she had the last name Scripps, Lida was not a direct relative of Ellen, who did so much for San Diego, and the trust fund relief did require direct relationship. However, another member of the Scripps family, Robert Scripps, came to her aid.

There is no record of what Lida did with Edelweiss, or to it, while she owned it, or who actually lived in it.

WRIGHT, MONROE, THOMAS & GLENN
ATTORNEYS-AT-LAW
SOUTHERN TITLE BUILDING
SAN DIEGO, CALIFORNIA

FRANKLIN 1571

April 12, 1934

Mr. W. C. Crandall
La Jolla, California

My dear Mr. Crandall:

As Mr. Harper is away, I am writing to you relative to Lida Scripps, who was badly injured Saturday evening by an automobile. Her leg was broken in two places below the knee-cap and she is now at Mercy Hospital. She is in need of financial assistance. I visited her yesterday and while she is quite cheerful, she will undoubtedly be confined to the hospital for a number of months, as she is about 78 years old and there is no prospect of a speedy knitting of the bones.

A provision is made in the will of the late Ellen Scripps for a relief trust fund which is available to any person who is a lineal descendant of Miss Ellen Scripps' grandfathers, William Armiger Scripps, or Edmund Saunders. I do not know that Miss Scripps is a lineal descendant, but I think she is. She naturally is timid about applying for assistance, but if anyone deserves assistance at this time, she does.

I know that some time ago she borrowed money from the First National Bank with which to pay taxes, and secured the loan by a first mortgage on the property on the corner of A and India Streets. Miss Scripps, as you know, is very deaf and I had great difficulty in conversing with her, but she made me understand she was worrying for fear the First National Bank would foreclose the mortgage by reason of the non-payment of taxes which fall due this month. However, I have taken care of that matter and the bank has assured me that it would not foreclose in view of the emergency which has arisen.

I am therefore writing in behalf of Miss Scripps and ask you to send me the printed form of application for

---

Mr. W. C. Crandall
#2
4/12/34

relief under the trust fund provided in Miss Scripps' will. I have called up Tom Scripps and he will examine the family tree tonight and let me know tomorrow if Miss Lida Scripps comes in the purview of the provision I have just referred to in Miss Ellen Scripps' will.

Anything you can do for her I am sure will be greatly appreciated not only by herself but her friends, of which I am one.

Yours very sincerely,

LAW:B

Leroy A. Wright

Leroy A. Wright

April 23, 1934

Mr. Robert P. Scripps,
Miramar Ranch,
Miramar, Calif.

Re: Lida Scripps.

Dear Mr. Scripps:

Several days ago, Lida Scripps, who is 78 years of age, was injured in an automobile accident at the corner of Washington and Goldfinch Streets, San Diego.

Senator Leroy A. Wright wrote me asking if she came within the meaning of the Relief Trust. He advised me that at the present time Miss Scripps was financially embarrassed, and that she is probably in for a long tedious time in the hospital. He stated that some of the relatives had arranged for taking care of her immediate bills, but that she is anxious to make a loan so that she can take care of indebtednesses already incurred and the indebtednesses that she will incur on account of her mishap.

Miss Lida Scripps owns the corner of "A" and India Street and a mortgage is held by the First National Bank against this property. Senator Wright arranged with the bank to extend time on this mortgage so that she is not in any immediate danger so far as foreclosure is concerned. This is the only piece of property that she owns that is not clear. Miss Scripps owns a number of pieces of property in San Diego City and County, and also property in Iowa and Illinois. She has been getting her income from the farms in the middle western states, for the most part, but this income has been cut off during the last two or three years, and she has found it increasingly difficult to keep her taxes paid.

Senator Wright told me that he had advised her several years ago to sell certain pieces of property for which she had received offers, but she had consistently refused to do so and now realizes that it places her in an embarrassing position.

I have not seen Miss Scripps as I found that things apparently had been taken care of so far as the immediate problems were concerned, and thought it best to wait until your return to find out whether I should go into this matter or not.

Very truly yours,

WCC:AR

W. C. Crandall.

The elderly Lida Scripps had friends looking out for her, as shown in this correspondence.

49

24
Fairgrounds & Racetrack

Right up the road Del Mar townsmen got a grant from the Works Progress Administration in the mid 1930s to build the San Diego County Fairgrounds north of town. The project brought welcome jobs to Del Mar. During construction an oval track for harness racing was added. That fact of a track sparked interest in the ritzy sport of thoroughbred horse racing.

Bing Crosby, one of the founders of the Del Mar racetrack, takes the first ticket from Mrs. Richardson, who drove down from Long Beach for opening day, July 3, 1937.

Glamor snapped back to Del Mar when Hollywood movie star and Rancho Santa Fe resident Bing Crosby, with Pat O'Brien and friends, bought in and founded the Del Mar Turf Club. The San Diego County Fair opened in 1936, the racetrack in 1937.

Opening day, 1937: The Crosby/O'Brien Hollywood connection brought movie star chums Barbara Stanwyck, Brian Aherne, Bruce Cabot, Jeanette MacDonald and Fred Astaire to Del Mar by train on the "racetrack special." They stayed in the luxurious updated Stratford Inn, the Hotel Del Mar.

The very next year another famous name came to the track: Seabiscuit. The still famous racehorse won a match race by a nose and set a new record. From *Seabiscuit: the Saga of a Great Champion* by B. K. Beckwith:

> It sounded like a natural — North America against South America — father against son. . . . It was to be run over the mile-and-one-eighth distance for a purse of $25,000, winner take all. . . . One stipulation which the Del Mar management insisted upon was that no public money should be bet on the race.
>
> On the afternoon of the match twenty thousand people packed the little course. Special trains ran from Los Angeles and San Diego, the highways were black with cars, yachts rode at anchor in the nearby bay, and fifteen planes dotted the track

Barbara Stanwyck and Robert Taylor were among the Hollywood celebrities at the racetrack on opening day.

In a match race at the Del Mar racetrack on August 12, 1938, Seabiscuit (top, and in front below), owned by Charles Howard, was matched with the Argentine champion Ligaroti, owned by Bing Crosby and Lin Howard, Charles's son.

airport across the San Dieguito River. Excitement ran at fever pitch. All Hollywood turned out to back the movie-owned horse. They organized cheering sections and carried large Ligaroti banners. The day was exotic and torrid, and the race itself was titanic.

Later, Lucille Ball and Desi Arnaz, Jimmy Durante, Bob Hope, Mickey Rooney, Bud Abbott and Lou Costello, Betty Grable, Raquel Welch, even J. Edgar Hoover came to the track as celebrities still do today.

Lucille Ball and Desi Arnaz at the racetrack with jockey Joe Philippi

J. Edgar Hoover and jockeys at the Del Mar racetrack

25
Wartime at the Fairgrounds

During World War II the fair and races closed and the facilities were used for military efforts. An airport east of the fairgrounds was used as a blimp base. The U. S. War Department took over the entire fairgrounds from the state. Del Mar Turf Club turned itself into an Aircraft Division, where airplane parts were assembled. Del Marians blacked out their windows, kept watch over the ocean for foreign ships and submarines, and made room in their homes for officers, enlisted men and their families.

The end of the war was announced at the Del Mar racetrack August 14, 1945. The fair and the races reopened the next year.

At Edelweiss, Lida Scripps held title till her death in 1944. Given the dismal description of the house in 1933 by Bill Arballo, Lida's age and financial upsets when she took ownership, her injuries and the lingering effects of the Depression, the house was likely left in limbo.

One of the operations set up at the fairgrounds during World War II was the making of tail assemblies for the B-17 bomber being built by Douglas Aircraft in Long Beach. Shown here are long-time Del Mar residents Marge Dunham and Mary Marquez.

26
Owners #5 & #6:
The Baker Women
1944

From June to November 1944 there was a flurry of baffling trans-actions as ownership of the house traded from one woman to another then another. The trend set by Lizzie Stelzner continued.

#5 Mrs. Henrietta Baker, a married woman, paid $1,500 to buy the house from the estate of Lida Scripps in June, 1944.

#6 One month later, in July, 1944, Mrs. Henrietta Baker sold the house to Mrs. Enriqueta L. Baker, a married woman, for $10. Strange. The ladies had the same last name and a variation on their first. Maybe a transfer to a daughter-in-law? In any case Mrs. Henrietta Baker took a loss of $1,490, at least on paper.

Mrs. Enriqueta L. Baker sold the house to Miss Marie Elizabeth Campbell and Miss Marion Agnes Ives, Joint Tenants, for $10 in November, 1944. At least the second Mrs. Baker broke even. Maybe there was a transfer of a larger sum, unreported for tax reasons? Or maybe not. I could not find the link between buyers that explains the chain of sales.

27

Owners #7:
Marion Ives & Marie Campbell
1944–1972

The seventh co-owner Marie Campbell had her singular version of the history of her acquisition of Edelweiss. Facts just get fuzzier. In a 1969 newspaper article in which she was quoted, Marie rewrote the record, saying that she and Ives, who called themselves sisters, gambled, got lucky and beat out several other bidders to buy Edelweiss at a court sale in 1940. The actual year on the title is 1944 with no indication of an auction. The article doesn't mention the price or how she came to know of the house or if she knew Henrietta Baker or Enriqueta Baker.

Memory can be tricky over 25 years (from 1944 to the time of the article in 1969), but Campbell's description of the house does ring true:

> "The porch was half rotted and weighted down by sea grass. The grass had even grown under the door of the front room."

She echoed Bill Arballo's account from 1933 (maybe they meant heavy weeds, rather than the kind of "sea grass" that grows in the water). Campbell said that a caretaker and his 90-year-old mother, no names given, who lived in the house, laid bricks on the floor in the kitchen, maybe to cook on, and burned a hole in the floor. Lida clearly hadn't made any improvements to the house. From Campbell's account, neither had Henrietta or Enriqueta Baker.

Campbell also asserted that Mary Pickford and Douglas Fairbanks as well as other silent movie stars held many gatherings "and at least one wedding party" at Edelweiss. Her proof of their presence there: "a two volume set of stereographic pictures of Italy with the bookplate identifying it as belonging to the library of Douglas Fairbanks and Mary Pickford." Not a lot of evidence, but...

Campbell and Ives were noted town eccentrics who cleaned the town's hotels and houses and sometimes sold candy they made in their kitchen. Marie, tall and tailored from the Midwest, said she had worked at Hull House in Chicago with Jane Addams. Marion, tiny and fussy, claimed to be of the Currier and Ives family and a descendant of Samuel Clemens, aka Mark Twain. The women drove a big old Packard car. Sometimes their two Mexican hairless dogs, who often wore outfits, joined them for rides.

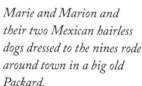

Marie and Marion and their two Mexican hairless dogs dressed to the nines rode around town in a big old Packard.

For Marie and Marion, Edelweiss was animal house. They shared the space with the two hairless dogs, additional dogs, monkeys, a goose or two, cats and probably others. Neighbors who were children at the time were at least a little afraid of the odd twosome and their spooky, animal-filled house: A monkey jumped on one child, another was chased by a goose.

As cleaners who had access to tossed-out treasures, they collected everything. The house was clogged. Pathways wound around and through high piles of books, newspapers, magazines, massive dark furniture, including an organ, brass musical instruments, mounds of more stuff, and the various animals.

They did have electricity. At some point they enclosed the open porch, using whatever windows they found, some matching, some not. Extras were rigged up to make that glass greenhouse on the east lot. They had a bird bath and furniture and umbrellas out front. They may have planted the cedar trees.

While Marion Ives and Marie Campbell and their pets occupied Edelweiss, both the house and the yard were thoroughly lived-in.

Then and now, at Christmas time the light glowing through the diamond-shaped cutouts in the wooden trim adds to the festive look.

Sometime along the way the women sold the lot on the west side. Marion died in 1969. Marie was in the house with her pets till she entered a convalescent home in 1972.

28
Owners #8:
James & Sydney Youngson
1972

Investors James Rodney Youngson and his wife Sydney Ashton Youngson gambled and snapped up the house and east lot from Marie Campbell's estate in April 1972 for $50,000. Youngson was the second man to own Edelweiss since 1885.

When they got a close look at the house, the Youngsons took what they wanted out and were deciding whether to sell "as is," take on the reclamation project or tear it down. A friend of ours who knew them heard about their quandary and asked if I'd like to see the house, just for fun.

29
Owners #9:
Back to Where We Started
1972–Present

When I saw the house in 1972, it looked about like it did when Bill Arballo saw it in 1933 but without the sea grass. And that's where this story started, back on page 1. We, David Maxey and I, took a gamble and bought the middle lot with Edelweiss on it for $30,000 in December 1972.

Artists' renditions of Edelweiss

Today 10th Street still has three houses filled with years from Del Mar's start, one of them perhaps not much longer for this world. A Torrey pine to the west is huge, majestic. The California pepper trees grow gracefully, and we do have jade plants. The cedar trees are gone.

We, the Maxey-Allison family, maintain the original order of the house. Within, our walls are still the rough-sawn redwood tongue-in-groove boards, the floor Douglas fir. It feels a bit like living inside a tree and offers wonderful acoustics to musicians.

A view of the house today from 10th Street looking south

We continue to tinker, updating the interior, redesigning the front and back garden spaces. We sometimes dig up various animal bones, horse shoes, shards of glass and pottery, relics of the past owners whose spirits may all linger.

Many guests, family, children and grandchildren stay in the house and the minuscule mansion. We are here for a while.

Juliana Maxey-Allison and Brad Allison at home at Edelweiss

ELIZABETH ZUSEV

We have made the house our own while preserving some of its history. Shown above is a view north through the living room and out the front door to the enclosed porch.

In the dining room we saved a three-inch-wide floor-to-ceiling strip of the Victorian-era wallpaper applied directly to one of the redwood planks of a dining room wall.

65

Outdoors are spaces to be enjoyed by both people (the deck, top) and chickens.

"The mansion" and gardens

Illustrations

Below is a list of the artists and other sources who have contributed the drawings, paintings, and photos that appear on the pages of this book. They are listed alphabetically, with the page numbers where their illustrations appear.

Most of the illustrations are also identified where they appear, either with the artist's signature or with a credit that runs alongside. In some cases of group projects, we couldn't identify individual artists.

Photos that aren't credited are from the Maxey-Allison family archives or are in the public domain.

Nicolas Charney archives: 3

Del Mar Elementary School Sixth Grade Class of 1996: 62

Del Mar Historical Society archives: vi, 4, 10, 13, 14, 17, 19, 36, 37, 38, 39, 41, 42, 47, 50, 51, 52, 53, 55

Del Mar Surfcomber (see "Sources" on page 69): 59

Dennison Library at Scripps College: 49

Friends of Barbra Dillenger: 26

Rick Ehrenfeld: 44

Kristina Krefting: 25

Abigail Maxey: front cover, i, iii, 6, 8, 15, 23, 29, 30, 31, 34, 39, 40, 59

Isabella Maxey: 38

Pucci McGill: 28

Operations Santa Fe (see "Sources" on page 69): 9

San Diego County Recorder's Office: 11, 12, 21, 32, 33, 45

Seabiscuit: The Saga of a Great Champion (see "Sources" on page 69): 52

United States Library of Congress: 43, 46

Bruce Vernon: 58

Elizabeth Zusev, 26, 63, 64, 65, 66, 67, back cover

Artists and sources retain the rights to their individual works. For contact information for an artist or a source on the list, please get in touch with the publisher:

Dayton Publishing LLC
P. O. Box 1521
Solana Beach, CA 92075
858-254-2959
publisher@daytonpublishing.com

Sources

The following resources were helpful as I researched the life of the beach house called Edelweiss, the people who lived there, and the way they lived. I list them here in case you would like to dig deeper into the history of Edelweiss, Del Mar or the world beyond. — *JMA*

Books:

Bill Arballo. *Del Mar Reflections: A Personal History of Del Mar.* Del Mar Media Group. 2004.

Merle Armitage. *Operations Santa Fe.* Duell, Sloan & Pearce. 1948.

B. K. Beckwith. *Seabiscuit: The Saga of a Great Champion.* Westholme Publishing. 2004.

Iris Engstrand. San Diego: California's Cornerstone. Sunbelt Publications. 2005.

Bill Evarts. *Torrey Pines, Landscape and Legacy.* Torrey Pines Association. 1994.

Nancy Hanks Ewing. *Del Mar Looking Back.* Del Mar Historical Society. 1988.

Elizabeth Whitfield Richards. *Del Mar Decades: A History of Del Mar, California.* Santa Fe Federal Savings & Loan Association. 1974.

Journals, Memoirs:

"The California Southern Railroad and the Growth of San Diego, Part II." *Journal of San Diego History, Volume 32, Number 1.* Winter 1986.

Kenneth C. Reiley. *New History of Del Mar.* City of Del Mar Archives. 1969.

Alice Rainford Memoir. San Diego Public Library, California Room.

Newspapers:

Del Mar Surfcomber. August 30, 1986.

Del Mar Times. September, 1997.

San Diego Evening Tribune. December 24, 1969.

San Diego Union. September 6, 1885.

San Diego Union-Tribune. May 10, 2009.

San Dieguito Citizen. December 11, 1969.

Interviews:

Bill Arballo. 2009.

Ernie Bertoncini. 2009.

Esther Lorraine Bertoncini. 1974.

Barbra Dillenger, Michael Makay. 2008.

Internet:

www.brainyhistory.com: 1885, 1886, 1887

Original Deeds of Sale:

Anyone can go to the San Diego County Recorder's Office and get copies of documents. I started my search there, sifting through many documents. I then ordered a title search from the Security Title Insurance Company. They could pull out the information more easily than I could.

Index
Color indicates pages with illustrations

70

About the Author

Julie Guenther grew up in West Los Angeles, graduated from UCLA and moved to New York City, where she got her first job at a magazine and met David Maxey. The Maxeys moved to and from New York City, first to Washington, D. C. and back, and then to Del Mar and back. Julie returned to Edelweiss with her husband Brad after many years in New York City, where she wrote for magazines — among them *Ladies' Home Journal, New York, The New York Times Magazine* and *Self,* and then sold Manhattan real estate. Her children, Brian and Elizabeth, both live in Seattle.

Dayton Publishing LLC
P. O. Box 1521
Solana Beach, CA 92075
858-254-2959
publisher@daytonpublishing.com

CPSIA information can be obtained
at www.ICGtesting.com
Printed in the USA
LVHW071038110819
627230LV00014B/994/P